Praise for the Poetry of I

"Lucid , raw and honest poems refrain that slide with grace and wit from the particular to the general, from past to present and back again, authentic and absorbing."
   - Rudy Wurlitzer, novelist and screenwriter (*Pat Garret and Billy the Kid* and *Little Buddha*).

"A fun sly jumble of poems that often tackle weighty issues..."
   - Jonathan Ball, *Winnipeg Free Press*

" If you ever get caught in the subway between stations, try to sit beside a guy like the guy who wrote these poems."
   - David Gilmour, novelist *(The Film Club, Back on Tuesday).*

"I enjoyed these poems immensely!"
   - William Peter Blatty, author of *The Exorcist*

"The best poems in Darrell Epp's After Hours remind you of the first time you got stoned. The first time you felt danger. You know how you felt the first time the veil came down. The first time you saw behind the wizard's screen.
                    Welcome to a new Oz!"
   - Michael Dennis, author of *Bad Engine* and *Low Centre of Gravity*

*"...*a gripping collection that tours readers through the seedy underbelly of Hamilton, Ontario and into the unconscious of the disenfranchised. Epp explores the unexpected graces that may rain down on us unawares...in his patron saint of the underachievers I think he has achieved something quite wonderful."
   - *Canadian Literature*

"...Epp explores diverse themes and imagery firmly rooted against a gritty postmodern backdrop."
   - *The Hamilton Spectator*

Mechanical Monkeys

Library and Archives Canada Cataloguing in Publication

Title: Mechanical monkeys / Darrell Epp.

Names: Epp, Darrell, 1972- author.
Description: Poems.

Identifiers: Canadiana (print) 20210102330
                Canadiana (ebook) 20210102349

ISBN 9781771615525 (softcover) ISBN 9781771615532 (PDF)
ISBN 9781771615549 (EPUB) ISBN 9781771615556 (Kindle)

Subjects: LCGFT: Novels.

Classification: LCC PS8559.P72 M43 2021
                DDC C811/.6—dc23

Published by Mosaic Press, Oakville, Ontario, Canada, 2021.

MOSAIC PRESS, Publishers
www.Mosaic-Press.com

Printed and bound in Canada.

Cover art and interior Illustration by Gord Pullar

ONTARIO ARTS COUNCIL
CONSEIL DES ARTS DE L'ONTARIO
an Ontario government agency
un organisme du gouvernement de l'Ontario

Funded by the Government of Canada
Financé par le gouvernement du Canada

 Canadä

 ONTARIO CREATES

MOSAIC PRESS
1252 Speers Road, Units 1 & 2, Oakville, Ontario, L6L 5N9
(905) 825-2130 • info@mosaic-press.com • www.mosaic-press.com

Mechanical Monkeys

by
Darrell Epp

 **mosaicPRESS**

Other Works by Darrell Epp

Imaginary Maps (Signature Editions, 2009)
After Hours (Mosaic Press, 2016)
Sinners Dance (Mosaic Press, 2018)

*"I worked too hard for my illusions
just to throw them all away..."*

-Axl Rose

*"I worked too hard for my illusions
just to throw them all away..."*

-Axl Rose

Contents

Love is Magic 1

Wolf Man 2

Fragmentation Grenade 3

Phantom Stranger 4

Fire Ant 5

Shimmer 6

Pregnant Fly Dead on my Windshield 7

Dofasco Dawn 8

Steel: Requiem 9

The Stars are Winking Goodnight 10

My New Career 11

While You Were Out 12

Minimum Wage Dollarama Express 13

Cinderella Suplex Summer 14

Juggling with Chainsaws 15

Sharing my Concerns with Customer Service 16

Against City Council's Decision to
 Widen Rymal Road 17

Food Bank Friday 18

Golden Willows 19

In the World of Things 20

Postcard from Babylon 21

I Worry About Dorothee's Leukocytes While Dark
Armies Advance 22

Paper Anniversary 23

Twilight of the Super-Heroes 24

Account Verification Required   25
Bird Brother   26
Waiting for the Flood   27
Slow Learner   28
Sinner's Prayer   29
Crowns for Everybody   30
Canticle for St. Francis   31
Zinnia   32
Gentrification Simulation Sleeping on the
  Balcony Blues   33
Lines Written in Dejection   34
Night of Black Glass   35
Two Smiles   36
What That Star Was Trying to Tell Us 37
Things That Matter   38
The Mystery of Flight Re-imagined as a Legoland
  Bouncy Castle   39
Intake Interview   40
Runaway   41
Broken Mirror   42
Outrageous List of Demands   43
A Durand Memory (1998)   44
SOS Without Reply   45
Desert Igloo   46
Bark   47
Secret Garden   48
An Onion   49
Waste Management   50
Yew Tree   51
Iris   52
Ode to Scars   53
Bloody Love Letter   54
Space Dogs   55
Outpatient   56

Sweet Poison	57
Seed of a Rose	58
Miscalculation Ode	59
Exit Wounds	60
Soul Factory	61
Cootes Paradise Walkabout	62
Peach Physics	63
Looking For a Kiss	64
Death of the Sacred	65
Shotgun Blues	66
Song for Ezra	67
Late Angel Sonnet	68
Practice Resurrection	69
End Times Daydream	70
Digital Resolution	71
Years Ago	72
Antibodies	73
Lemonade	74
Infestation	75
Life Jacket	76
Snow in July	77
My Favourite Century	78
Water up to My Knees	79
Greeting Cards for Non-Existent Holidays	80
Legend of Atlas	81
Mechanical Monkeys	82
A Good Neighbour	83
Lines Written on Poe's 210th Birthday	84
Let Me Make Myself Clear	85
Ecstasy	86
Acknowledgements	87

Love is Magic

we suffered from a lack of common reference points.
i mean, her mother was a witch. mine
sold cosmetics to her friends, carved
sandwiches into perfect tiny triangles.
no one wanted to burn her at the stake.
but who wouldn't love a witch in the
house, especially if hollywood's
been telling us the truth. failing
grades mysteriously born again
as a-pluses, club feet and sour
milk for everyone who looks
at you funny, the chest-swelling
pride that comes with the secret
knowledge. Maybe when you
get to the end you start fresh
with a new baton, new maps,
new paintings on the walls
of the motel six. or maybe
just an inkling, a lottario
ticket and the sound of your
own echo as you sing your
way out of the hall of mirrors.
hello walls. i wish you were a door.
watch me now: i've been practicing.

Wolf Man

my shadow was a wolf that looked like dad.
the atmosphere wore a white medical smock.
a mad scientist peered down the barrel of the
double helix and created a lab rat with giant
mastodon tusks, just to prove he could do it.
that look you gave the waiter could morph
sand into glass but your bracelet should be
worth a lot more now since we murdered
the coral reefs with sewage and plastics.
that's the good news. the bad news is
on his way. or already here and lurking
behind an artifical palm tree. sometimes
i think my voice sounds like a robot.
one day i'd like to wake up a human,
and fully alive. there's a few things
i'd have to do first. we gave a meth
head a dollar, wondered where his
tribe will go when gentrification
makes us all real estate millionaires—
dunnville? out past the grand river?
the hypodermics were in full bloom.
heavenly arms rocked us like a mother.
once upon a time there was a girl.
we held each other in the dark.

Fragmentation Grenade

gave gerald the 40 bucks but he never
gave me the two caps he promised,
just old jokes and crackpot theories
about gravity strings and leprechauns,
subcutaneous microchips and falling
angels. i'd still prefer the two caps.
i want hard results, an explosion in
slow-motion reducing me down
to a gaggle of singing shrapnel. so
much for summer's hydrocodone:
lick the bag, make a wish. a ghost
is always stuck in that moment
before the paint dries, that hour
before the luggage clears customs.
squeaky cloud cogs. sci-fi lego sky.
bramble and thistle sabotaging the
construction site. stuttering pirate
parrot. the courtoom drama's
shocking twist, the beat cop
just looking to make the quota.
how close we come to mystery,
with only algorithm standing
between being human or a
burger king beef cow! moo.

Phantom Stranger

the day we forgot to protect our passwords
there was all this beauty we missed out on:
the fruit from that quince tree, tiny and tart,
rolling along the sidewalks, into the gutters;
shadows like vampire capes caressing the
lawn, smiling when you don't particularly
feel like it is beautiful, so is light on red
barns, light biding its time out behind the
salvation army where men patiently wait
for a free hot meal. a cannibal dictator
cries over his mother, an ex-girlfriend
goes crazy trying to fix everything all
at once, revenge festers like cankerworm,
like abu bakr al-bahgdadi still seething
over spain's *reconquista* of andalusia,
the husband so dumb he's still keeping
score. beauty's like a phantom stranger
lurking behind potted plants and always
the last to leave the party. we fought
over money while rust ripped the door
right off its hinges. spun right around
by american ghosts and facebook likes,
a hand reaches out, ties it all together,
that's beauty: eternally she calls to us.

Fire Ant

walking past the statue of our founding slaver
the gears and cogs inside me keep it down
to a low hum, rise up to a steampunk
clanging screech when we pass the
food basics where bananas are 49
cents a pound because chiquita corp.
propped up dictators, tore down the
rain forests are here we are: fat yet
still hungry, tied into boy scout knots
over 2 for 1 specials and pension plan
formulae. the beams began to sag,
even the wallpaper grows sinister,
the words of the spell that would
set it all right are long forgotten.
even on holidays fire ants work
so hard, the mass production
tickles the amygdala like a
big brother with a mean streak.
cracked-rearview caliban; air
pregnant with tornadoes. turns
out the old maps got it all wrong!
greenland isn't nearly that big. the
southern hemisphere got a raw deal.
there's falling angels everywhere.

Shimmer

dorothee falls asleep with her palm on
my belly, her shoulder blade carving
the air like a dolphin's dorsal fin as
it kisses the ocean, the sky, the future.
what a day we had! oldtown, newtown,
fused into a joyful electric smudge,
distant condo towers mingling with
the ragwort and milkweed valiantly
cracking the pavement. the spooky
quantum entanglement of the dusky
purples and carmines left us baffled,
horny. a veteran asked us for a smoke.
a dead newspaper caught an updraft,
took flight, those inky marks of
politics and panic stamped on its
pages like the babblings of b-movie
lunatics. all the stars of libra burned
just for us. mars loped erotically
toward jupiter and we almost forgot
about the moon, such a tiny sliver
of shimmer. the 7-11 glowed like the
beacon of a fairytale lighthouse. a
squirrel and her kittens peeped out
hopefully from under the dumpster.

Pregnant Fly Dead On My Windshield

the smear like a microdot of jam, i watched it,
wondered about her family, wondered if she'd
even known what hit her, with a brain only a
microscope could see. the crossing guard
barely registered, just another clown with
a whistle, the christmas lights were out so
no one cared about drone strikes in yemen
and nobody would until disney bought the
movie rights. pro tip: get morgan freeman
to provide the down-home gravitas, you'll
need it when only the dental records abide
unmelted. down in the top-secret basement
the remote-control pilot gorges on red bull
and pride. the long-range sniper dreams of
his mother. his mother says he's her hero.
straight-a students invented a new way to
ignore the still small voice, the fork in the
road. picture the earth as a snow globe in
a black-and-white movie, ringed by angels
and antimatter playing quantum billiards
for all the marbles. i'm just trying to be
helpful. picture a narrow path. picture
a rumour of another way, insistently
haunting the billionaires' barricades.

Dofasco Dawn

tiptoeing along the rusty catwalk, jittery from
the night shifter pills, i thought it was the sun
but it was a glowing slag heap waiting its turn,
somehow i got everything upside down again.

we transmuted mineral resources into products,
chased the ace, counted cards, hypnotized
ourselves in the flickering arc lights, the
blowtorches of the tig and mig welders,

sold our souls for a ponzi scheme. map and
territory, word and idea, bound together with
knitting needles and yarn—the holy pulse
behind it all, i felt it, and the spaces between.
somehow i got everything upside down again.

Steel: Requiem

dreamed of crazy eights back at the tin mill.
dreamed we still had a tin mill, but now
it's cheaper to roll slabs in brazil, or
almost anywhere but here. head office
is in luxembourg, or mumbia, it's called
amalgamation, the planetary consolidation
of steel. my hand still hurts from comicon,
the cosplay parade slowed down traffic,
i was in a mood, punched in my hazard
lights and started picking fights with
masked avengers, obese klingons. lucky
if i don't get sued. and my real anger
wasn't for them, it was for our blind
technocrats herding us off the stage
to join the neanderthals, leaving all
our strivings as a legacy for unborn
cyborgs. coal dust from the mines,
just diamonds under pressure, like
re-training for customer service or
hunting for scrap metal and copper
because the pension fund's insolvent.
natural gas fires carve out a memorial
tattoo. the arc light's prism still calls
to us like the song of the sirens.

The Stars Are Winking Goodnight

my eye like a strange balloon
loping towards infinity, a lone
bedbug dreaming in the cushion
of the couch, a colorado potato
beetle in a frankenstein mask
climbs the ladder, rings the bell,
because neoliberalism's out of
time. that last stimulus package
was a real wet rope, if you know
what i mean. let's try it again,
with enthusiasm. concentrate.
throw on a few more zeros,
pretend we've only just begun.
i have two eyes but don't count
on lefty, he's stuck in the past,
sees nothing but high school
crushes and greedstruck scooby-
doo villains playacting as
poltergeists for the inheritance,
for the insurance, for the hell
of it. i used to pay bills on time.
then i lost the plot, hit snooze
like a sun with a dead battery.

My New Career

behind the toxic vault of sky, ghost galaxies
spin so slowly that it's hard to tell what
brand of shredded mozzarella is the better
value. juggle grams into pounds inside my
head while raytheon bombs wipe out whole
bloodlines without ever trending on twitter.
the planets we could have colonized if we
hadn't opened door number three! the
wish-granting genie that picked my lock,
slipped behind an altostratus cloud while
i complained to the manager. no refunds
or exchanges without proof of purchase.
the customer used to always be right,
now he's a swing voter arguing with
the screen at the self-checkout and
begging the simulation for a hug.
the human resources manager called:
i said, who needs a welder with shaky
hands, or a star that refuses to shine,
they thought it was just a smudge on
the lens before they counted the
gravity waves. so many grudges
and mismatched mittens out there!
without love, it's all just paperwork.

While You Were Out

...and the centipedes were weeping because
of low bandwidth speed, and their idea
of a classic film differed from that of
netflix. the silverfish behind the fridge
were buzzing like old-time cathode ray
static, modernity's mask began to crack
and peel in the heat, somersaulting
spiders assembled their battalions
into the shape of an arrow pointing
at the clock with the dead batteries.
where the filth met the sky, angelic
dispensers of grace, and in the
dopamine-stoked half-dark, a
questioning glance verging on a
smirk. out behind mission services,
holy fools in a 5g panopticon,
zombie carnies juggling debits,
credits, and chainsaws. dorothee
shouldn't leave me alone this
long; i always end up sniffing
parking meters and debating atm
machines with hegelian dialectic.
still i kiss the mystery under a
raging congress of constellations.

Minimum Wage Dollarama Express

hailstones on the roof making
that popcorn popping at the
tuesday matinee sound, the
bus driver chugging zip fizz,
the scarified rider remembers
her last kiss, panics, wonders
when the next one will come,
i try to read but i'm stuck on
page 17, the stone in the river,
nestled in a collar of foam, i
just can't picture it, like stars
aborning and dying without
ever telling me and even my
dreams involve punch clocks.
all those middle managers i'll
eternally regret not punching
in the throat and if i could i'd
push the button, blow it all up,
start again, change my name to
tarzan, ride the barton to the end
of the line but if i miss my stop
i get a second warning letter
from the boss's nephew. don't
ever tell me my vote matters.

Cinderella Suplex Summer

dreamed of cinderella's ghost, the
angels' highway between memory
and desire, woke up in the basement
wearing hip waders and a clown nose.
all that summer there were germs outside,
and flash flooding and locusts in kibuye
and no one cared how many a's you got
back before benzodiazapines colonized
the medine cabinet. all those souls,
frog-marched out of town by the white
lab coats, a few stragglers, coiled up
in the fetal position and babbling like
rivers. when i stocked the ice cream
french side out so it said *vanille*
instead of vanilla the employee
of the month screamed at me
but it was only one letter's
difference so i didn't think
that was very fair. and desire
like fire, desire like a suplex
that leaves you breathless. the
sun ejected radiation that curled
my shingles but still my prayers
never made it past the ceiling.

Juggling with Chainsaws

the problem is all the unsolicited free advice.
scars i can handle, scars buy sympathy,
scars teach humility by scrawling human
finitude's calling card on the epidermal
wall, scars turn weary mauve with age,
their jagged edges filed down like the
erosion-battered blue ridge mountains
until all the pain's in the rearview like
distant barns on fire. scars make me
scream and dance and gasp at the sting,
all those sweet things the dead can't
do, so don't tell me how to do it
your way. even heard of a guy
who used foam rubber replicas
in rehearsal, saved the black and
deckers for the pay-per-view
but i always wanted life to be
an endless wire between alpha
and omega, a house of cards
built from trick questions and
wrong numbers. your mileage
may vary. gravity's a bitch.
check the plugs, lube the teeth.
never let them see you sweat.

Sharing my Concerns with Customer Service

 in the shadow of the american cross
between the buying and the selling
ever feel like some lecherous force
has retconned you into a puppet?
if so, press 1, and an agent will
be with you shortly. between ralph
lauren and hot topic i turn to stone,
feel the whitecap breakers of envy
and lust, ride the waves like a
cork in a tsunami, distracted by
shiny things and tiny rows of
jealous algorithms. behind the
mellow bon jovi muzak i hear
lucifer laughing all the way down.
they're widening the expressway,
asking the poor to pay for it. and
butterflies on hamster wheels,
backward-talking marionettes
evicted from the dream due to
incomplete paperwork. when
i stopped screaming the box
factory was a condo and the
credits had rolled on my
happy ending years ago.

Against City Council's Decision to Widen Rymal Road

am i really the only one who finds traffic
jams sexy? the steaming commuters,
the steaming radiators, hyundai horns
reminding me of gideon's trumpet,
old testament judges and new age
oracles begging you to hit the like
button. an ambulance punches its
way through the collector lane,
her siren heralding occlusion,
infarction, or pulmonary edema.
its doppler effect reminds me of
an ex-lover's face i haven't
touched since o. j simpson's
slow-speed chase, and the way
astronauts are never the same
after the heat shields buckle
upon re-entry. some join a
monastery. some sell shoes.
some retreat to cabins in the
high sierras, scribbling out
their manifestos, manic as
mantises they fill their blank
pages, they know space is
vast, final, and so very cold.

Food Bank Friday

the robot guard-dogs scrabble sideways,
sniffing out the obsolete, their rfid tags
with the long-gone expiry dates. soviet
space dogs still whiz around above our
heads, long after sci-fi became sci-fact.
the wind-carved faces glow vermilion
in the snarling trash can fire while we
wait in line for a cheese burger, a
pepsi, a bag of chips. the demazenod
door behind st. patrick's—all it took
to wind up here was one week of bad
luck. but everything is brother to the
flashbulb glare of this holy minute,
everything is all right here, together,
even the bed bugs that pit neighbour
against neighbour, you can gas them
but they're a part of the sacramental
world-pulse too. so is your enemy,
so is lack. a woman with a hacking
cough pushes her way in front of me
and i smile, there's food enough for
all, just don't touch the trophy, the
trophy is mine because i swam
through fire to get here.

Golden Willows

the wheels came off our some-assembly-required
elysium gradually, then suddenly, and where
to stash all these toothpicks, all this surplus
copper wire? i just looked down to check
the time and when i looked back my
favourite glacier was gone, gone as
the jurassic, melted down into a pizza
huts' drive-thru window. tied my shoe
and it was all boarded up, padlocked,
haunted. at least the breeze was still
sweet, scuttling crabwise along the
desjardins canal, rattling the branches
of the golden weeping willows and
how i wish those willows could talk.
the redness of her bra as she diced
the onions, and the way the hulk
has no one to talk to about his
daddy issues, just green screens
of rage jamming the signal, it was
my blood she cleaned up when i
dropped the bowl, later she drew
me a picture to calm me down,
count up my atoms, hear their
song: this poem is for dorothee.

In the World of Things

my werewolf stalker takes his time,
he knows i'm not going anywhere.
the calendar says today is ascension
sunday but the elevator still smells
of marlboro reds and stubbing your
drunken toe on the coffee table
hurts no matter how many bible
verses you memorized. the old
man's cataract-clouded eyes
see through the world of things
into the phantom zone, where
ghosts bloom extra heads on the
hour—i try not to interrupt.
domestic violence across the hall,
but i can't tell if it's real or tv.
burning spanish galleons on the
horizon, and pirate booty buried
in quicksand, the dark angel of
certitude, her mask beginning to
crack and peel in the infernal heat.
solar quanta burnish the afternoon.
i grab the day by the throat like a
lottery winner, feed the wolf on
the wellspring of my heart.

Postcard from Babylon

thanks to stupidity and fear's lonely duet
we can't have nice things. movie butter
isn't real butter these days, everything's
plastered with warning labels and even
my dreams are copyrighted by disney.
you can't get within 100 feet of noah's
ark anymore because of all the tourists
hacking off souvenirs for their walls.
got some nice shots with the telephoto
lens but it wasn't the same. we paved
more ground to alleviate congestion
but it didn't work, now we just have
more time to fume under glass and
miss the fireweed, the lilacs, the bees.
all those hardworking pollinators
sacrificed to the god of progress—
ever think maybe they just invented
paradise so they could sell all those
'no trespassing' signs? the truth was
on no screen nowhere. the truth was
a spy behind enemy lines. the truth
was as welcome as a leper as we
counted up our assets, parcelled our
resentments into tiny faberge boxes.

I Worry About Dorothee's Leukocytes While Dark Armies Advance

the goldenrod remorselessly encroaching
on the fallow brownfield, some purslane
and milkweed , the sign promises upscale
bohemia but the real estate developer ran
out of credit so weeds riotously reclaim
the future from a fast-talking hipster with
the double-parked lexus and i'm not sure
how i feel about it all. we were already
late, the line was down the hall, finally
they jabbed and poked looking for a
vein until the rn asked me to leave.
dorothee's white blood cells are low
and no one can tell me why, stars
keep on burning, galaxies keep on
grinding, she insists on the generic
iron pills because she's frugal, she's
always been that way, our first date
she explained her philosophy about
tipping, i was permanently hooked,
the way she angles her head while
choosing her words is like a super-
power, creeping thistle, buckthorn,
saw them too, as city council debated
what to do with my beloved ward 3.

Paper Anniversary

i love your nose and i love your nose more
than any other nose in the world, would
rather stare at your nose than cure stupidity
or win the daily grand. told you this while
a couple celebrated their paper anniversary
by wordlessly throwing pizza crusts at the
seagulls. the couple wore matching jerseys,
a quixotic, unrequited love for the buffalo
bills strengthened their matrimonial bond.
my depth perception was hurting, no far
or near, just jangly caffeinated electrons
sparking against the light, a polychromatic
obscuration that made me want to celebrate.
we shared a burrito as the condo developer
maxed out his line of credit, even left
the spade in the ground, ran back to
his mother's oakville mansion, stone
lions out front, indoor pool out back.
electrons everywhere, but electrons
didn't tell the whole story. later we
argued about a murder mystery's
weak third act, the fingerprints on
the gun. still my luck held like
a flower blooming in a storm,
a victory dance in a burning barn.

Twilight of the Super-Heroes

some super-powers are cooler than others.
knew a guy who could squeeze his tears
into diamonds, burned out his tear ducts
trying to make himself cry 24/7. bob
could melt into fog when you rang a
bell but it still hurt when caitlin ran
back to her parents, took the dog,
left the bills. just like magic i can
come in last in any marathon, but
it still hurt when the barber asked
about a bald spot i hadn't known
i even had. no tip for him! spent
so long on hold my toenails grew
into talons, ripping their way out
of my shoes. gravity nailed me to
the floor with one hand, juggled
quasars with the other. powerful
idiots made me dig a hole, fill it
back up with new dirt, lemon-fresh
and certified organic. stood at the
edge of the world, maybe, couldn't
tell, it was too hard to see. i said
to the fog, bob, is that you? no,
fog said, this time it's only me.

Account Verification Required

for your protection, the machine freezes
your accounts until you can prove who
you are. but who knows your zip code
from 8 addresses ago, or your password's
favourite password? the shadow knows,
he's always right on time with the snide
remarks and coulda/woulda/shouldas.
and that puddle—one lonely dorito
drifting so slowly—could have been
a glacier with a bit of practice, and
not just another lousy first date, she
picked at her salad, scowled at my
jokes as i sopped up my sweat with
a monogrammed napkin. that was in
the past. the present's where the real
danger lurks—clone war veterans
gone rogue; the downsized, afraid
to love; ancient and sacred reefs,
choking on single-use plastics.
tried playing a bait-and-switch
on my neurotransmitters: that
worked, until it didn't. tried doing
cartwheels all the way home: turned
out i hadn't lived there for years.

Bird Brother

we are all somebody's wind-up toy, with
accessories sold separately. panicked
when i couldn't remember my last good
deed, then it came to me: last week i
didn't step on a pigeon, thought she'd
just fly away when i got close but her
wing was broken, she just stared up
as i made a clumsy course correction.
so i stared up too, hunted for clues in
clouds, friendly faces in victorian
windows, secret knowledge riding
on the breeze. telepathic communion
with my tapeworm is one thing but
no such luck with co-workers, their
nuclei are far too unruly, you might
as well try praying in a mosh pit or
setting all your scarecrows on fire to
hold back non-hodgkin lymphoma.
city council poured raw sewage into
the marsh, told us to conserve water.
big shots made big deals while i fed
the pigeon sesame seeds. under the
city was another city, under that was
a song, poking through the heat wave.

Waiting for the Flood

dorothee says we need to talk about the
upstairs toilet, the flapper seal has a
slow leak, our water bill is too high
already, my pulse auto-corrects and
i want to kiss the toilet in gratitude—
i thought it was something important.
like those murder hornets everyone
just stopped talking about, only so
many disasters allowed on the
carousel, i suppose, and what if
martin's right and it all comes down
to a newly-discovered fragment
of the gospel of judas? ancient
creeds in need of revision, all
of history just a game of broken
telephone, leaky kettles, leaky
rowboats of dime store pirates,
and the way super-villains always
explain their mad plans instead
of just getting on with it. pull
the string! light the fuse! it's
like you're miles away, she
says. it's such a thin thread
that ties my soul to the earth.

Slow Learner

the shortcut to school took twice
as long, and lord cthulhu ate my
homework. an extra week's
detention for not showing my
work when i carried the 7, all
i cared about was getting the
right answer, rinsing off reality's
clown make-up, seeing what
really goes on under the hood.
such a sensitive child—even a
pillow could leave scars. all
those whirling dust motes
trying to cut me, do the math
and it's all a bit much, like
late-night crazy glue that never
works the way it does on tv.
the world's weirdly wired,
still there's coneflower and
sage bursting through the
concrete like an anthem.
hearts of stone *can* break,
you just need patience and
steel-toe shoes. behind it all,
one true thing, burning like fire.

Sinner's Prayer

the lonely contrail of an airbus a-310
bisects the day. bermuda sounds
nice right about now. vagrant, we
stagger through a furious cloud
of midges. groaning fire escape
hanging by a single bolt—porn
shop sign, its incandescent
stammering like a fatal regret.
millionaire twerker shot in foot
is trending, a celebrity argument
got out of hand. internet gossip
smothers the mystical like a fire
blanket, should i try the sinner's
prayer? someone says 'vote,'
as if perfect penmanship could
stop a runaway train. there's
talk of cloning extinct monsters
from dna they found in an iceberg—
i think i've seen this movie before.
i say that a lot lately. all these hints
of the unknowable other, i collect
them like pokemon. stir the pot
with a wooden spoon as our culture
boils, howls, and turns to steam.

Crowns For Everybody

monday's bursting with strange jugglers.
carved into the picnic table in woodlands
park: I HEART RUTH SORRY I BROKE
YOUR JIB PIPE. discarded cellophane
achieves escape velocity, burns the retina
like a magnesium flash. the city founder
dug out a home here in 1780. some days
i feel like writing him a letter. objects
and their names diverging, spirits
hovering above the bay, jenga-style
syllables, something about a narrow
way, and don't run with scissors,
act your age, remember to diversify
that portfolio, hard to hear above
all this progress. the radius of the
rot swells, pushes against the tides
until the tides push back. drunk on
grace, the distributor of crowns
anoints us all, regardless of the
labels on our underwear, the
prescriptions behind the mirror.
still so many mummified! wake
up, friend, from your cardiac event.
take my hand. bite down hard.

Canticle for St. Francis

trucks ramming into the speed bump like
a demented metronome until i start
screaming curses backwards just
for a change in the laugh track.
still i believe change is possible:
look at st. francis, look at glaciers.
now you see them, now you don't.
he stripped naked at city hall to piss
off his rich dad, got carried away,
wound up blessing every blade of
grass, every grain of sand. 2020's
a long way from assisi but i try
stealing his moves, kiss the air,
the guano-stained statues of
hard-charging generals, the
abandoned strip mall waiting
for her luck to change. the
future—all those golden hours!—
chartered, parceled, subdivided
into family-friendly lots. hard to
resist the weight of all this commerce.
a wasp—swear to god!—landed
on my monitor like a conquistador
and i almost forget to breathe.

Zinnia

is reality a cube or a football or a holographic screen?
you'd thnk we'd have some consensus by now. but
we can't even agree on tomato/tomahto, or how
to fold the quilt. ever since the global reset i
find myself in the strangest places: time
machine phone booths, drained edwardian
victory fountains, or reflected in the eyes
of minecraft-addicted zombies. hacking
through diaphanous membranes of dream
with my swiss army machete—where's
my pocket defibrilator? and where did
all this tinsel come from? the cicadas
hush when we get too close. bumblebees
fight it out among the lavender. words
i'd give my arm to take back, and how
i lost my parking spot with just a single
spin of the wheel. smirks instead of salutes.
turns out my rocket ship was just an elantra
with a good imagination. head back
when we get to the bankrupt pet store
covered in christmas lights in august.
the star-shaped zinnia seeds in my
palm are real, i cast them to the wind,
tremble with delicious suspense.

Gentrification Simulation Sleeping on the Balcony Blues

only the crows remain
still i miss the falcons

the lost blizzards of
our heroic pioneers—

still they ask, still we say,
no comment, wait for the beep.

Lines Written in Dejection

from ancient oceans
my me asks of me
(amid tinseltown's
hypnotic howlings)
what has happened to
the g.i. joe soldiers
of our stale-dated
pentecost, and why
is he running so
late, the bionic
saint you promised me
we would one day be?

Night of Black Glass

…and my four walls like four black mirrors.
there's a breeze from my hands' frantic
waving but no reflection of me at all—
was that last blind date a vampire?

and why was that x-ray machine so cold
reminding me of my rebellious body when
freedom from the burden of representation
was what i wanted like divine forgetfulness,

not this burden of measures and co-ordinates,
salsa doritos on the breath of the intake nurse,
my birdbones gone hollow, transparent now,
no fingers left for the black mirror to point

back at me, tap the glass, it ripples like waves,
that last barbeque, all this i wanted to tell you.

Two Smiles

that last drone strike hit me right in the feels
but two strangers smiled at me on the way to
duarte's deli and that kind of made up for it.
drowning in gold and baffled by forgiveness,
we choose diet poison instead of regular like
we're doing the oncologist some big favour,
dream of trips to bahamas, cuba, or tattooine
but chicken out and don't go anywhere, don't
even move a muscle or pace the room envying
the guy who won big on texas hold-em but
look at his eyes, his hands, i know he's lying,
like i lied when i said we were almost there
but i was so fearful back then, and that was
even before droids incinerated families eight
time zones away. one of the smiles came
from a psychotic off his meds and one came
from a jehovah's witness trying to make her
quota but still. duartue's hoagies are the best:
they have a framed letter from the mayor to
prove it. thick ropes of sausage hang from
chains. raw organ meat swims in tin pails
like the suitcases of the damned. steak's on
sale but that's not what i want: they know
why i'm here, they even know my name.

What That Star Was Trying To Tell Us

maybe there's no right answer. i mean,
maybe we're both wrong. like that last
election that was no real choice at all,
just two pixellated puppets dancing
to the plutocrats' tune. or unlimited
viewing options promising to deliver
happiness but in a shocking third act
twist leave us hollowed-out, tin-man
style, brainless, gutless and begging
for another hit. not heavy enough to
burst into a nebula-birthing super-
nova, an old dwarf star winks once,
goes dark, like a dream when the
dreamer wakes up. rain washes
away our defiant chalk drawings.
nerdy binary code swaddles the
globe in press releases from royal
dutch shell, gazprom, vodafone.
we follow the river's meander
hoping she remembers the way,
visit dad in the home, he thought
we were spies until we fed him
smarties one by one, sucking so
slowly, saving the red ones for last.

Things that Matter

dorothee laughs at nothing. of course
not, there's no real nothing, not with
us all huddled together like hamsters
on wheels, eichmanns-in-training in
uniform cubicles. that's neither hide
nor hair, suck it up butter truck, six
and one half dozen mothers, fee fie
fo fum like your refrigerator's hum,
a first-world lullaby while yemen
burns, or starves, depending on the
the two-headed coin's capricious
flip. and most of the cosmos is still
missing! they call it dark matter.
does it matter? not the way your
late period matters. and whatever
happened to those toffy wafers
with orange in the middle that
oma fed me, i can't find them
anywhere. dorothee spits up at
the norad satellite. algorithms of
lust feed the bitcoin blockchain.
is it too late to say sorry, sorry
for voting, sorry for the baby
teeth i traded in for dimes?

The Mystery of Flight Re-imagined as a Legoland Bouncy Castle

this is the heron i pray for during
morning ablutions during
nocturnal humiliations
her hollow-boned mass
equals energy sleeping
between her wing and
the weed-pocked earth
her twin telescopes
scan for cracks where
life might hide—how
regal her updraft glide!
but king kong to iron
man isn't progress
neither is raytheon's
patented heat-seeking
missiles or communion
with grape juice. i
smashed the x-wing
fighter out of spite:
now it's too late for
sorry and all the
furniture's been
rearranged. st.
jude respond to
my text with the
winking emoticon.
if not for me, do
it for the heron.

Intake Interview

why can't we *all* be superheroes? it seemed
like a reasonable question at the time. then
came the white-smocked pharma-pimps
preaching better living through chemistry.
and baffling menus of counterproductive
choices when all i wanted was scrambled
eggs and a car with interstellar overdrive
just like president eisenhower promised.
or was it superman who promised that,
his kryptonian-accented words echoing
through his castle made of diamonds?
you're acting awfully presumptuous
with regards to my neurotransmitters,
doctor. eighty per cent of friendship
is in the not asking. take the hint.
look at crutches, look at glue, they
do their part just fine without words.
oops! you flub your lines, break the
spell: how about i be the doctor,
you be the mad monk? transplants
for everybody! new hearts for old,
lilac blossoms for palliative's felt-
tip pen, and cyberdine terminator
houseboys picking up the pieces.

Runaway

pulled weeds. dreamed all night about waking up,
what a rip-off. forgot to read the fine print, found
a stranger in the trunk of my rented ford fusion.
now his problem is my problem, according to
the laws of *omerta* and warner brothers inc.
my grey matter's no joshua tree, resolute in
all kinds of weather, it's more a wellesian
montage of dirty harry, die hard and dad.
like the teen sidekick believing his mentor
will always arrive in time, save the day,
return the hateful freak to arkham asylum,
i wanted to know what we were like before
we had minds or thoughts or even bodies,
just dreams of lights in the one great light.
so i skipped out on the spectral ancestors
waiting to grill me about my poor choices,
the untucked shirt in all the family photos,
didn't even leave a note or water the fern,
packed a suitcase, drove through a starry
blizzard until i found her, hugged her like
a python, counted all her fingers and toes
like it was a liturgy, gassed up the tank,
she navigated our way out and cried
when the sun arose to kiss macnab st.

Broken Mirror

it was only a minor disaster, thanks for asking.
no category 5 hurricane with a girl's name,
no buffalo wings without the hot sauce, but
it still hurt when the mirror stopped working
and you thought we'd turned vampire in our
sleep, you always had a flair for dramatics,
maybe that's why i stuck around for so long.
stared at the nothing in the glass while the
russians replaced the president's brain with
a manchurian replica. or was it the martians.
oh to be a blue whale with a nine-foot penis,
carried away by the song of my brothers,
pitch-perfect and heartbreaking. a million
pounds of krill a day and i'm still hungry.
oh to swim with the mermaid queen and
arrive fashionably late at the poshest party.
oh to be inside the snow globe inside the
black and white movie that won all the
critic's choice awards. outside, the street
swelled with protestors like a hysterical
virus. jostling air molecules produced
heat and doubt. a bug-eyed evangelist
quizzed passersby about the meaning
of life and the hard road to salvation.

Outrageous List of Demands

the face was a mask but the pain was real.
hated the way you said 'spiritual but not
religious,' your injudicious punctuation.
that's the last apostrophe you'll misplace
in this house, my dear, the basement's
already full of them. the attic's flooded
and i'm sick of hurricanes named after
my cousins, try rivers instead, try ice
cream flavours, we could all use extra
minty swirls in our front page disasters.
prairie chinook of my grandfathers,
rearrange me. rebuild me out of
lego, save me from the experts,
their prescription pads and cruel
calculus. capture bliss, package
it, retire to the grand caymans.
once i stubbed my toe looking
at a meteor. once i thought i
understood you but not fiat
currency, albert einstein or
electricity. there's still an
angel inside every light
bulb, dancing just for us,
that much i'm sure of.

A Durand Memory (1998)

purposeless, so homeless, so couch-surfing
and locked out after midnight, our jittery
hero looks everywhere in vain for a key.
nothing to do but tighten up his scarf and
wince at the fact that there are some things
you can never get ahold of: bacon fat
sizzling in the pan, the kisses he missed
because he was dreaming and mother
never even told him. when the house
next door exploded because of a natural
gas leak and the explosion didn't sound
like it did in the movies he almost wrote
a mad letter to his elected representatives.
it's snowing now, with polaris blinking
through the blizzard wall. it's beautiful:
what if all the beauty in the world was
right here, he thinks, what if i could
squeeze it in my hand like a slushy
snowball? he blinks, yearns for an
angel's eye view of himself, his
dime store clown shoes. the cold
seeps through his parka, reminds
him of his ancestors in old photos,
scowling toward sinister haystacks.

SOS Without Reply

a winged unicorn should never stop believing
in life on mars just because it's tied up to a
parking meter and it's out of coins and here
comes the by-law enforcement officer.
a poem should be a window to reality:
break the window, win a prize, play
again, with fingers sticky from too
much cotton candy. some contestants
may find the truth dripping down the
veins of maple trees planted by your
pioneering ancestors. they collected
the sap, thought it cured hangovers,
they built a barn in a single day—
we can barely put our grievances in
alphabetical order without running
after the main west 5c express bus.
history was a drunknen clown, the
moon was a half-eaten ice cream
sandwich. the alien mother ship
was out of range: our frantic cry
for help choked on the attic's pink
insulation. and the nestle company
killed off the chipwich because
they didn't want the competition.

Desert Igloo

it's not easy building igloos in the sahara.
the sun melts the ice, and wind grinds
even the hardest monuments back into
powder. ten thousand years later you're
back where you started. it wasn't easy
listening to the doctor say words like
biopsy, inconclusive, false positive,
post-op physiotherapy. wasn't easy
telling dad about how you dropped
the ball, sold out for a pension. the
pension fund went bankrupt anyway:
bad investments in venezuelan hotels
just before inflation went to 30 000%.
it's hard picking lint off your pants
with even the most powerful magnet.
harder still watching them buy the
land right out from under our feet,
turning even the noble gentry into
squatters, rootless renters. our new
overlords have bmw's with sunroofs
and even their eyebrows are sexy.
easy was a warm bath with epsom
salts and a fresh pack of razors. not
everyone gets to go home a winner.

Bark

out past cygnus a star was dying. died, i mean:
its last light left home back when noah's ark
was standing room only. stars don't hurry.
imagine if our hearts beat once a century,
maybe we could put down our burdens of
me-first and limited-time offers. i am mainly
water but there's 77 cents' worth of gold
running through my veins, i know, i
googled it so it must be true, picture a
supernova's engine running on fumes,
raging against the dark, that's where
everything comes from, where new stars
are born as death gives way, surrenders
to life, the promise of a new morning.
this morning burleigh counted birch
trees in gage park because one-by-one
was what he needed and after the pro
dog walkers left he stood on his hands
to look at the white papery bark from
a fresh angle, relief rained down like
a divine liturgy, his wounds no longer
mattered, even the dutch blight
didn't matter, furiously infecting
trees older than confederation.

Secret Garden

for veronica's sake, prairie sunflowers
planted by the electric fence in front
of the canola oil processing plant, a
jade tree left by orlick industries tool
and die, hostas in the windows of
the old westinghouse plant— millions
of families filled their homes with our
appliances. and rumours of wizards
tripped up by their own magic spells,
paralyzed, rooted to the spot in mute
warning against flying too high. a
talking book that contained merlin's
locks and keys, wise king solomon's
memories, his signet ring of power.
maps of the human heart carved on
a puzzle box bursting with levers
and switches. and tips for turning
enemies to dust, dreams into iron,
lovers into legends, impervious to
time's chittering minions. no luck.
still you check the classifieds, the
gossip at the carlton tavern, aching
for a bunker, a refuge, for you,
veronica, and the sunflowers.

An Onion

i wasn't sad, just slicing an onion. still…
there were things worth crying over.
all that runoff from the chicken farms
shut down the beach due to e. coli
bacteria. port dover's a long way
to drive for no swimming. moses
not entering the promised land,
only squinting at it from a distance,
after those long years of wandering.
the men of the salvation army hostel:
lost, written off, zero social media
presence, one reminds me of moses
vs. amalek, king james version only
please, arms raised in victorious
benediction, keeping them up,
fighting fatigue, the devil, asking
for help, frantically now, echoes of
dad in every twist of the maze,
and he never knew, never got
to hear about the mark he made,
maybe it would have helped him
fight if he'd known lymphoma
didn't get the last laugh, and i
wasn't sad, just slicing an onion.

Waste Management

that photo of you french kissing ronald
macdonald by the eastgate square walmart,
that i kept, but not the mahogany dresser,
not that hideous wrought-iron sculpture,
i dragged all that to the curb for the road
warriors, the scrap metal scavengers
with wagons hitched to their ten-speeds.
let them melt it all down, squeeze some
value out of our failure, and the broken
dracula jack-in-the-box, that wasn't
garbage, it had sentimental value, i
chased the garbage truck all down
tisdale, crying and dying for a light
in the black, even the light of sinking
ships burning on the horizon, i'd have
dug up the whole landfill, that's how
desperate i was, and we could have
been missionaries, role models to
our nation's youth but something
vital was replaced with bedazzled
simulacra from the home shopping
network. o to be recycled into flame!
mad max peddles harder now, under
the burden of his newfound bounty.

Yew Tree

but if time's a cube then behind some secret door
it's still 1997, the cops were brutal that year,
that was before cell phones and dashcams,
one cop put a gun in my face just because
i lived next to a chop shop, thought i knew
something i didn't, three of them beat their
batons on a bleeding man on the sidewalk
in front of show world just because he was
drunk and anonymous. i saw it all, am still
seeing it all. smirking bullies who left me
tongue-tied, the perfect comeback arrives
decades behind schedule, they've all
moved on to costco memberships and
family-friendly vans, trading gloriously
feathered mullets for sweaty comb-overs.
they're long gone; i'm rooted to the spot
like that 8000-year-old yew tree on the
discovery channel. still remember a hot
safety on a mustard-coloured mercury
topaz, drinking and driving and crying
to the end of the queen's highway,
st. christopher and alice cooper riding
shotgun, just to admire the buffalo
skyline, salute her immortal architects.

Iris

…and the cop directing traffic in the hailstorm
is the cop who threw you in the back of his car
because your photo didn't match your face,
you'd had a beard back then, and dreams,
is the cop who taught you traffic safety
in the 80's, they named a park after him,
actually just the northeast quadrant but
it's a big park, and putin punking nato
is gord at the end of the lane taking your
bike out for a spin, he said he'd be right
back but you waited until nightfall and
he never returned. his dad called your
dad. treaties were signed. mustard gas
briefly blinded hitler in the trenches;
clouds of killer nanotech mowed
down syrian school kids during the
rose bowl. you always were a slow
learner. emperor titus, crucifying 7000
rebels just to burnish his resume, is
the cop who chased you just because
of a skateboard and a dead kennedys
t-shirt. it all runs together when there's
blood in your eye, flooding the iris, and
martin changed his number years ago.

Ode to Scars

to be forever throbbing was the whole point
of the endeavour, even the mountains are
moving in dizzy loops and whirls, even
stars dance and star dust is what we are.
so we tangoed, saluting the furnaces that
forged us. we stole a truck, just for a
night. returned it with a full tank after
pulling figure-8's in the football field.
how like a flower moon was your face
that night; i should have held on a
little tighter. cutting deals with rats
and laughing like tomorrow would
never come until our cogs and gears
began to let us down. balanced on
one foot, reaching for the switch,
something popped and i wound up
on my knees but not praying, just
moaning at the bottom of the stairs.
black rainbows of bruises cuff my
shins. pain is a cruel teacher but i
still say yes whenever i can. on special
occasions i shout it out loud like a river
falling off a cliff. oh the things we could
do before our bodies were temporary!

Bloody Love Letter

my poor wife! all i ask of her is telepathy,
maybe some antlers, the ability to eat
glacier and spit out flame. lawyers on
radios say this happens all the time.
still i'm queasy about turning our
backs on the view off catalina. or
even a grub eating a leaf, nazareth
miracles on stained glass windows.
don't tell the starving children
about the buffet left untouched,
the five-star gourmet dumpster.
skies as plush as a child's toys,
mountainous clouds tumbling
down barton, farther down a
rust-coloured stain, relentless
as gangrene, and aldermen
building castles out of sand.
the sign says yield but i'm
too stubborn. in a frenzy
like before the evacuation
we take heat lightning
as a sign of the divine.
angels or mirages, go
ahead: surprise me.

Space Dogs

on our way back home the i -90
smelled of gasoline and monkeys.
i swear the joshua trees hated us.
silouetted against the raging dusk,
the wicked branches writhing like
cthulhu's own tentacles, it was
easy to believe they were ghosts
of suicides like in dante's goofy
inferno or a mythic monument
to joshua's genocide of jericho,
that's what the mormon pioneers
told their children. wanted to stop
at olancha but didn't meet the
dress code. the sky so clear
reminded me of those dogs
the russians shot into space
in tin can sputniks, quickly
martyred, now endlessly
orbiting, sons watching
their fathers in the rear
view mirror, hollywood
lied to them, just in time
a mojave thistle split
the ground wide open .

Outpatient

stay away from the windows. maybe they'll
take someone else, someone else's family.
and that math test you weren't ready for,
silently pleading with the nerd to see his
answers, you're still dreaming about it
decades later and if there's a lesson in
there somewhere, don't tell me what it
is. you could go to the farmer's market,
tap the watermelons, strip yourself
naked, paint yourself blue and still
nothing would change. walk across
niagara falls on a string, the by-law
enforcement officers will be waiting
for you. heard of a guy who invented
a way out, they bought his silence
with a trip to disney and a pension.
the laproscopy burrows into your
true self, reduces it to a field of
zeros and ones. tiny pellets of
titanium and cesium and we just
stood at attention out of respect
for the white lab coat. biopsies
turning castles to mist, the dreamer
waking, forever leaving us behind.

Sweet Poison

i'd be sad without chocolate but sadder if you
cut off my head and moved to california.
already you have most of me: my favourite
sweater, my a+ credit rating, that tooth i
lost chasing you down the stairs—my
rocketship's imaginary but take that too,
i'm feeling generous tonight. just tell me
if you see martians out there, so i can
finally stop wondering. it's no fun
being sad but happy couldn't live
without it, someone has to tell the
glutton the buffet's winding down,
to warn us against sugar but why
should a poison taste like heaven,
that's just not right. no flowers
without bees, no oaks without
armies of dead acorns. the dome
of the sky, how it tastes like
tungsten filaments, just before
the sun shines and shines.

Seed of a Rose

thought i'd finally got on top of things
but then i heard about those two black
holes eating each other out in the centre
of the galaxy and all bets were off.

this is your brain. this is your brain
on fire. this is a rose, with height,
width, the whole nine yards.
imagine it! before thorns drew

blood, before subterranean
roots clawed at the sun, a
seed lonely and dreaming
in a world gone ravenous.

and my seatmate back from gatwick
drinking too fast and ranting about
area 51, his stories didn't add up
but oh how i loved him,

at least he was dangerously alive,
his mind wasn't owned by disney.
after the fourth bottle of claret
he told me i was beautiful,

told me the captain was a lizard.
only his fire mattered, not the
facts, nor the arcane physical
laws that kept us from crashing.

Miscalculation Ode

the mad scientist forgot something.
a critical rounding error and human
progress tumbled down a blind alley.
canada post mixed up the test results:
congratulations! or, not. a barn owl
howled and fritz dropped the brain,
replaced it with the worst possible
choice. almost found a novel way
of saying 'nostalgic for elephants'
but a purple sandpiper banged into
the glass, gripped the ledge like a
die hard action hero. i panicked
and hit the wrong key, now it's
time for string searches through
ghost files and oolong chai
with honey from local bees,
they feasted on milkweed
while we voted for crooks
or cyborgs, democracy's
a powerful placebo. and
the hackwork the critics
called a masterpiece, its
howls of crucified outrage
echoed through the gallery.

Exit Wounds

that coniferous forest used to be a strip mall.
i mean, dimes used to be real silver, and
christmas trees weren't always made out
of taiwan plastic. is that an apple orchard
or a drive-thru pharmacy? ever since
they cut out the easy overtime it's been
getting hard to tell. told myself I was
prepared for anything but naah, just
another story, like how astronomers
lied about the stars: it was all just
tinsel and confetti the whole time!
and the stink that overpowered you
when you looked for a summer
sublet, it's appalling what some
landlords get away with. you
cried, even called city hall.
steven seagal filmed a movie
here. the high speed chase was
just a slow lap around gore park.
the redwoods were balsa wood
props and what if the whole
world's like that: a patchwork
replica held together solely by
the strength of our affections?

Soul Factory

caught in the crosshairs of geography and time
garlic on my breath benzene and ozone in the air
the frantic cicadas rioting in the brownfields
the lake's boggy stench almost comforting now.

the carp glare up accusingly—the water's a stew
of corrosive dyes, solvents, oxides and polymers,
leaving me pining for the good old days, before
words got in the way. specifically, infancy.

a googlesecond before the arrival of langauge
the soul blinks, grieves the impending loss,
now comes the treachery of facts and objects,
the hard work of remembering how to run

like innocent light, or just pout in the corner
for threescore and ten, there's always a choice.
like that rich guy who sold out the ironworkers,
he could have taught himself how to say no.

his yacht is hanging up in drydock, or maybe
he took it down to grand cayman, who knows,
but the midges are murder this year, one wrong
move and you're in the middle of a swarm,

trying not to choke makes it hard to remember,
harder to forget the story of our own legend:
lonely marathon runners looking for a way
through a maze of digitized question marks.

Cootes Paradise Walkabout

the tallgrass prairie is howling and throbbing
with chittering cricket armies. see a pelican,
see an endangered jefferson salamander,
terminally lose it when a gooey snickers bar
wrapper entwines itself among the singing

whitewood asters, their bouquets really do
look like seedling constellations but that's
still not enough, not this far from easter.
gone are the warblers, gone as dial-up
modems, gone as blockbuster video.

pine for a miniuature resurrection while
a red-headed woodpecker taps out a coded
message on an encrypted channel. woodland
voles, racing for the shadows: between their
frantic leaps, all the eternity you'd ever want.

Peach Physics

never even tried an avocado until I was 30, can you
imagine?
somebody get me a lawyer. how about that old guy
with the grey suit who always reveals the real
killer exactly 90 seconds before they run the
credits? he's on right after wheel of fortune.
still no anti-gravity belt pack, no elevator
to the clouds. still waiting for that secret
identity, complete with flying talking car.
and lime-flavoured kisses at the drive-in,
that's all over, so says the caterpillar
earthmovers and wrecking balls of the
fast-talking land barons, the mayor
with his tightly-clenched writs of
demolition. they even paved over
an orchard! all those knotty peach
pits making new trees and feeding
millions in an alternate universe, if
the latest quantum science holds up.
you can still give thanks for birch
trees or the furnace grumbling
reliably under your feet, but who
knew how much I could miss a
single magpie, a norman castle, and
who knows when I'll see cardiff again.

Looking For A Kiss

mud. midges. summer soon. again. now.
then. and the century's last leaf riding
on air, the whitewater downdraft of the
51 delaware rosedale bus. an x-ray tech
apprentice carves a heart on the frosted
glass with his finger, he's looking for a
kiss, a reason, an explanation airtight
as math, tied up in a polka-dot bow.
how to sleep upside-down, bat-style,
without headaches, how to walk
a straight line without being drunk,
and that time on star trek spock grew
an evil beard, traded logic for larceny,
what was that about, black holes,
worm holes, fm radio static scrambling
the transporter beam, a rounding error
in the boiling cauldrons of antimatter,
if only he could remember, and kirk
still couldn't beat him at 3-d chess,
some things never change, like how
they turn into mannequins when he
squints, terminators when he blinks,
the bus detours down the mouth of
a lion, in spite of which, still no kiss.

The Death of the Sacred

augie said he hated cops but he'd call the cops
for help when he got ripped off on a ten dollar
dope deal, sometimes he was calling 911 four
times a month. said he hated the government
but the government paid his bills, i told him
that didn't compute but he wouldn't listen.
he had the confidence of a sociopath, just
like that guy in kentucky with his noah's
ark replica, bigger than the astrodome and
featured in people magazine. i believe it's
wrong to charge money for noah's ark but
nothing's sacred since captain kirk blew up
the enterprise. he had his reasons but so did
everybody: the *genocidaire du jour*; the guy
who changed the coca cola recipe, renamed
real coke as coke classic; the studio honchos
who let fat affleck play batman—he's a ninja
detective, not a pouting slumming trust fund
baby! and fighting war with war, whose bright
idea was that: harvard man or princeton man?
prayed for a miracle but second verse, same
as the first. and even the jehovah's witness
detours around my house like the sign says
quarantined, zombified, highly contagious.

Shotgun Blues

the mailmen deliver bouquets instead of
bills and my co-workers are all cylon
spies until a possum foraging through
my recycling bin wakes me up. not
for the first time i pray for a shotgun,
a shiny winchester '73, but that's a
rifle, not a shotgun, i must be sober,
let them call the by-law enforcement
officers, i can't win with those guys
anyhow. passed out with the movie
on pause and burned a crystalline
martian landscape onto my retinas.
feel my way to the fridge, the milk,
lean up against a load-bearing beam
like samson the blind judge, raging
and loving and losing and winning.
it all reminds me of how ifrah awale
would carve infinity signs in the air
to punctuate her sentences, those
lucky nitrogen and oxygen atoms,
savouring the arc and whorl of her
fingerprint, the geometry of soap-
bubble-delicate digital bones, riots
of song roaring out of her hands.

Song for Ezra

i said 'ezra' because i thought it was the cat,
but it was the sun waiting a billion years
just to tickle my cheek with strands of day
like a warm ghostly spider web, growing
stronger now, gently defeating the night
like an incoming tide of bashful tsunamis.
her tiny particles are models of politeness,
she's not like her big brother orion, her
big sister cassiopeia. birth order is very
important; there's no escaping it, like
childhood mistakes you can't stop
paying for, the standardized aptitude
tests you treated like a joke
more all of the aboves and i'd
be designing a new space station,
living on easy street instead of
cannon st. the hurting brother
we lied to; of course we had
spare change: who doesn't?
still she shines with baffling
generosity. ezra means *help*
but i wasn't asking for help:
tomorrow began and i
thought it was the cat.

Late Angel Sonnet

the new terminal manager says he's found
'efficiencies' – that can't be good news.
his door is always open. he likes
brainstorming and teambuilding.

i want to sue my guidance counselor for
malpractice or laziness or just for that
stupid moustache: a smirking phys. ed.
teacher pretending he was magnum p.i.,

king stud on the island of maiu—
the 80's, that was a strange decade.
my angel's running late. i need him to
baptize this post-black-friday monday

before it's desecrated with market-tested
jargon, trademarked logos and fancy fonts.

Practice Resurrection

…still it soothes us, the clanking and humming
in the half dark, the giant sooty bellows of the
coke ovens, the sky sucking on smokestacks
in a new-wave science fiction sort of cpr.
and the drones aren't predators, not yet,
so far they're friendly as the family dog.
super-heated mineral wealth, dark riddles
hidden in actuarial tables, interest rate cuts,
the heat radiating off the giant silos at the
canola oil plant, the ladder snaking around
the tanks of liquid air under the skyway.
cobblers' grandsons coding scripts for
financial derivatives algorithms, lego
figurines under glass, mementos of the
future's remorseless colonization. the
mayor lied, promised me he'd stand up
to the billionaires but i'm not bitter,
ever since the maternity ward i've
been expecting too much, fighting
the tides, the times, the second hand's
psychotically-cruel one-way trip. hard
to practice resurrection in the shadow
of such insect-like efficiency. learn
to pray, to plant a flower, and wait.

End Times Daydream

mighty mountains flattened into sheets
by divine mallets, the valleys exalted,
crooked paths made straight, the prophet
isaiah, still too classy to say i told you so.
panels of experts were hastily assembled.
they said new legislation might help but
i just saw it as an excuse to pull a weed,
kiss a stranger, hold a billionaire hostage,
donate the ransom to all the locked-out
steel workers. we waited too long: the
rocks cried out in deep bass hosannas.
the great beast of the sea 666-ed his way
around the globe and i just yawned: bow
down to the big dog, hear his mighty
roar, same old story. forget kingdoms,
i`ll take a library that still shushes people,
a do-over on that last meet with ifrah.
this time i wouldn't be in such a hurry.
mountains are big, and hard, you could
hurt your hand punching one but it`s
a trick, they're only atoms and atoms
are nothing at all, just electric charges
circling each other across vast empty
pools. that's all I remember from
school, that and serita, she told a
friend of a friend she had a crush
on me but that friend never told *me*,
serita switched lockers, skipped a grade,
married a dentist as a consolation prize.

Digital Resolution

the private eye sniffed at the crime scene,
even gave it a lick, desperate for clues,
the killer's musky spoor. there were
no suspects, which means, everyone
was a suspect. how about the prodigal
son, the jealous golfing buddy, no,
it has to be the grieving widow, a
blonde amazon shrouded in black,
nothing else will satisfy. yelling
at the tv is never a good sign.
on another channel a parasitic
larva thrashed inside a centipede.
and the crowds, so many people
filling the streets, celebrating or
rioting, turning, now pointing at
me, the spinach stuck between
my teeth. I said `no,' the echo
bounced back, there was too
much space, it should have
been out past centauri where
black holes were eating space
raw, not here, we can't speak
mystery's language, not since
upgrading to hi-def smart-tv.

Years Ago

night flung meaning at the spaces between the stars.
there was only one can of pringles ranch chips
for all of us but somehow we never hit the bottom.
no one remembered to give thanks for the miracle:

we`d lost the knack years ago. and two rodents,
chiseling away at the mortar between my bricks,
searching always for a way *through*, a way *in*.
their song, louder than the hum of the hard drive.

Antibodies

oily ravenshadow, spirographing higher than heaven,
even the stale-dated memory of it is enough
to turn my hands into deadly weapons,
with adamantium claws lurking under
the knuckles. are you into home remedies?
i use birdsong as a sort of inoculation
against postmodern slippery slopes and
unjust property tax assessments. and
when that kawasaki ninja 300 ran the
red at main and gibson, i just savoured
the doppler effect of its screaming
four-stroke, two-cylinder engine,
smiled like the t-800 terminator
strutting out of the fire, armoured
and glittering, after the humans
were sure they'd finally won.
past st. charles, past dollarama,
the urge to give that flat track
bully the finger but he's gone.
i pray instead, grateful for it all:
sparrows and finches, robins
and orioles, the gift of singing;
the sun, its light, baptizing
the world into wakefulness

Lemonade

ice cracking on burlington bay, that'll do it,
or sometimes just current events, sometimes
just lonely. it's late this year, blame sunspots,
blame gravity, blame that angry rip current
bursting from those two black holes
that merged three billion years ago.
or the dwarf lilac, bereft of blooms
and choking on the byproducts of
combustion. a stick: i drove it into
the dirt like a conquistador, like
armstrong planting his flag, tied
it to a drooping branch on my
lemon tree. i wanted it to stand
tall, its pregnant flowers heavy
laden with fruit and straining
sunward. i wanted a truce in
my war against the invisible,
antlers instead of ear buds,
someone to vote *for* instead
of just against, a trusty guide
when tiptoeing drunk down
the spiral staircase. and what
fyodor promised us: beauty
enough to save the world.

Infestation

the way you screamed when you saw
the pill bugs eating our strawberries
was enough to make me believe in
ghosts. and the bridge i use to cross
over desjardins canal, the site of
the great train disaster of 1857:
that too. an axle snapped and
the train jumped the tracks,
flipping over down onto the
ice. mayor's son, alderman,
bishop, millionaire: all lost.
stomping your feet doesn't
help. on they go, chomping
remorselessly, and if i had
an exoskeleton like they do
maybe i'd be just like that.
i don't have an exoskeleton.
i have an appendix but don't
know what to do with it, a
minimum wage guardian angel
and sub-zero celsius net worth.
the iroquois traplines are gone.
so is the studebaker factory. all
i know is: that's a lot of ghosts.

Life Jacket

all i ever wanted was everything so dutch tulips
went under the microscope, i wanted to decipher
their bulbs, pistils and stamens, moth wings and
sick babies' hearts, their lionhearted flutterings.

my dimestore candle's just a puddle of wax now,
still the light sings, pressing out against the night.
we sprayed the trees and poisoned the bees,
now my science fiction honey tastes funny.

it's a weird disease when bloodletting's the cure!
tried everything else: epsom salts and opium tea,
talk therapy and d-3, late night scams, now i'm
filling up blank pages until the fever crashes.

so we went down to pier 23 where they sling
chains around steel coils, and you blowing
out that dandelion was like saving someone
from drowning: that's how impressed i was.

Snow in July

sometimes the exhausting is in the pretending,
the dreaming of the arriving, and discarding
suitcases stuffed with cinderblocks and
how easy it was to dodge camaros when
we were under a mile-high glacier. that
was a long time ago. so was the 80's,
when the cheerleader in the slasher
film said, *i think we should split up
and go in different directions.* every
car at the drive-in honked in derision.
it was a double feature so i was late
getting home. to teach me a lesson
they changed the locks, grew old,
downsized into a burlington condo.
what a day for my dna spirals to
learn surrealism! clouds carved
out of plexilglass; the krautrock-
inflected rhythm of the aortal
valve, it's ghostly afterecho, the
glittering knives of cardiology.
encrypted in navajo code, hope
slips past the soviet censors
disguised as snow in july, or
the sun kissing the flowers.

My Favorite Century

hooray for hollywood! thanks
to that old-time movie magic
charlie chaplin is still and always
with baseless optimism striving
against modernity's hammer and
brother you wouldn't believe how
much i miss the 20th century.

sure it had its embarrassing
moments—hippies, the khmer
rouge, those golf balls alan
shepard left on the moon—
but what would you expect
from a century midwifed by
nietzsche and jack the ripper?

maybe you can't have einsteins
without hitlers, one senses the
dark and the light locked in a
symbiotic stranglehold, but
just think of the good: the
movies, the dumb ideas, the
super-sized super-value meals!

please tell me how you feel. i'm
sorry i lost my temper, i know
i'm too old for that but let's blame
it on the times, let's laugh at that
little tramp trying to eat his boot,
to wish his shoelaces into spaghetti
way back in my favourite century.

Water Up To My Knees

my feet sinking into sand,
the surly lips of a catfish
looking up at the uninvited
guest muddying up his turf,

as a jet-ski scares away geese,
ducks, pigeons, seagulls,
even a pair of swans, and
i remember with surprise

my grade three teacher who
gave me a week's detention
for my low math test scores,
even after I explained to her

look, i didn't mean to get a
low score, math just isn't my
thing, but she felt insulted
and she needed some revenge.

she yelled and screamed and
i was scared at the start but
by the end i felt sorry for her
and i did figure out all that

math stuff eventually, it just
took me a bit longer than most.
now the jet-ski is almost gone,
and the birds will come back,

they were here first. someone
waded through this water in
1920, 1820, 1720, 1620...it
feels nice to be a part of something.

Greeting Cards For Non-Existent Holidays

there's corn stuck in your teeth, loser!

happy birthday, world's greatest orphan!

everybody at work thinks you're a weirdo!

you're dumb, but you've got great hair!

Hallmark Corp. knows what you're thinking!

get well soon: we need that hospital bed!

it's not you, it's me! please don't call me!

(actually it's because you remind me of my mom!)

my condolences in regards to your recent genocide!

i've met rocks with more personality than you!

too bad about the layoff, please don't go postal!

so sorry your lousy cooking ruined our anniversary!

your face reminds me of a famous dictator!

congratulations, the facelift looks great,

you can stop looking so surprised now!

happy wrist-slitting monday!

oops, sorry 'bout the apocalypse!

where do i know you from exactly?

are you somebody important?

i'm looking for a co-signer...

Legend of Atlas

charging onwards and upwards,
upwards toward the light,

foraging in the gloaming
searching for shiny things,

eternal things, things that
never change. an

aphid on a leaf, chomping
like a glutton at a buffet,

new buds on the lilac bush
i'd written off for dead.

the sky's pregnant with
mysteries, I carry it on my

back, what a holy mission,
what spindly little shoulders.

Mechanical Monkeys

i kept my mouth shut, took the money, tried to
make my cubicle feel like home. years passed.
when my mind split open emptiness rinsed out
the day, rinsed out my eyes, everything looked
off-kilter, like how during times of stress life
can imitate paranoid cold war science fiction.
my supervisors were pod-people replicants.
local parks were landing strips for galactic
space cruisers. my lunch break was over but
i didn't go back, i ran, then leaped along in
hero-size strides, cataloguing new species
of flora and fauna: robot koalas, stainless
steel clovers, creepers, mechanical monkeys
living on credit and voting survivors off the
island. better you than me. call toll free to
choose your idol. meanwhile the sky had
gone out. the terminators had encased
us in a shimmering dome, they said it's
for our own good. we gave up too easy.
i pushed against the dome, calculated
its circumference, its diameter, started
searching for a person or just a string
of rebel neurons uninfected by the
nano-obey virus, someone who could
remember when there was all the time
and space in the world and villians
never won, at least not permanently.

Good Neighbour

looks like we both missed garbage day
two weeks in a row. i climb over the
bags piled up on the landing. he steps
out of his door, smirking silently. i
look at the garbage, return the smirk,
as if we're saying big shots like us
have more important things to worry
about than garbage. nice day, he says.
i look around and confess he's right.
he starts in with the small talk and
i don't mind. when it slips out that i
don't have a pistol he becomes
agitated, offers me one of his. i
politely refuse, he begs me to
think it over. his back porch is
filled with giant ferns. inside his
room a cat sounds unhappy. we
wish each other well. i start down
the stairs. nice guy, I think, he
smiles when he has to and in the
night when he fights with donetska
he tries to keep the noise down.
the stairs wobble and make a lot
of noise. visitors complain, say
they're dangerous, but I'm sure
they're safer than they seem.

Lines Written on Poe's 210th Birtdhay

starless nights, when the
regal curvature of her
smile is more than enough.

my happiness— hide and seek
has always been your favourite
game, you spoiled little brat. a

hand-knitted sweater. a hot bath
like swimming through a coma.
bug-eyed maniac, were you me?

the punch line is revealed as the
tragedy recedes from view. the
joke is on me and that's just fine:

i earned that bald spot. the spy of
time has defected, not even the
conqueror worm can scare me now.

Let Me Make Myself Clear

wanted erotic but they gave me erratic, looked
for something fun and real: they sent me to a
funeral! my ticket to paradise was a thicket of
paradox. and the paved shoulder on the 407
extension was littered with corpses, all those
baffled raccoons and possums robbed of
habitat and baking on asphalt, everybody
woud have cried if it was a disney/pixar
coproduction but when it's your own
windshield you learn to look the other
way. cruise control helps when every
radio is tax hikes, teacher strikes and
hotel california. hereos were villains
in disguise, our lovers were robots,
still we dreamed of high school,
of pushing a toroise through its
cavernous halls, mr. freisen's
baffling equations. at least my
brain's not floating in a jar of
formaldehyde in a mad scientist's
castle, waiting for the transplant:
hooray! dear publisher: when i
said i wanted my book to be read,
i wasn't talking about the colour.

Ecstasy

downtown's not the place for stargazing.
nothing up there but fuzzy moon, some
smudges, a crackling light bulb with a
stupid moth endlessly banging into it.

hear the sound of someone running,
someone shouting, replay the day,
wonder about tomorrow's trickery,
the air is full of mystery and waves.

suddenly it's there,
a pulse, a swell,
feel my face smile,
hear myself laugh—

as every thought in my
head turns into a prayer.

Acknowledgements

Many thanks to the editors of the following magazines, where some of these poems first appeared:

Mystic Blue Review
The Fiddlehead
The Stray Branch
Taxicab
Eunoia Review
The Arrival
Riggwelter Literary Review
The Wagon

Thanks to

Gary Barwin

David Collier

and
The Writers' Trust (George Woodcock Fund)

for helping out during a difficult time